# PHILADELPHIA

## A PICTURE MEMORY

**Text**
Bill Harris

**Captions**
Fleur Robertson

**Design**
Teddy Hartshorn

**Photography**
Colour Library Books Ltd

**Commissioning Editor**
Andrew Preston

**Publishing Assistant**
Edward Doling

**Editorial**
Gill Waugh
Jane Adams

**Production**
Ruth Arthur
Sally Connolly
David Proffit
Andrew Whitelaw

**Director of Production**
Gerald Hughes

**Director of Publishing**
David Gibbon

# PHILADELPHIA
## A PICTURE MEMORY

**CRESCENT BOOKS**
**NEW YORK**

Considering that both America's Declaration of Independence and its Constitution were ratified there, and that it was once the capital of the United States, indeed for many years the most important city, except for London, in the entire British Empire, it's a little sad to report that one of Philadelphia's contemporary claims to fame is that it is the hometown of Sylvester Stallone. It isn't that the City of Brotherly Love isn't proud to have produced the Italian Stallion, but it is even prouder of the great figures in its past.

With that in mind, Philadelphians decided to begin a new phase in the city's history by digging into an old one to mark the 200th anniversary of the death of one of these great figures, Benjamin Franklin. Strictly speaking, Franklin wasn't a native. He was seventeen years old when he arrived in Philadelphia from his native Boston, and he found his way there almost by accident. He had been a printer back home, and decided to go to New York to seek his fortune. There was only one printer in New York at the time, and he didn't need any help. But he suggested that there might be some opportunities down in Philadelphia. There were: a lot more than either of them dreamed.

Franklin was down to his last dollar when he arrived at the Market Street Wharf, and he decided to invest part of that dollar in a bit of bread which, along with a drink of river water, would stave off starvation for a little while. In 1723, the currency in Pennsylvania was different from that in Massachusetts, and so was the fare in the bakeshop Franklin found. Not wanting to appear a country bumpkin, he asked for three pennies' worth of bread, which to his surprise turned out to be three loaves.

"I was surprised at the quantity," he wrote, "but took it and having no room in my pockets walked off with a roll under each arm and eating the other." Soon after, he gave away the two extra loaves, partly because he had a charitable instinct but mostly because he thought the bread under his arms made him look ridiculous. Such is the vanity of a seventeen-year-old. A little later that same evening he wandered into a Quaker meeting house and went right to sleep. By the time he awakened he had decided that Philadelphia was to be his home and, throughout the rest of his life, he was as passionate as anyone on the subject of his adopted city.

He had no trouble finding a job, and by his second night in town he was working in Samuel Keimer's printing house. Within a year he had saved enough to go into business for himself, and his nest egg included the price of a passage to London to buy presses and type. At least he thought it did. However, he ran out of money in England and was forced to work there for eighteen months to raise the price of a ticket home. Home was, of course, Philadelphia, where Keimer was willing to give him back his old job, probably pleased not to have Franklin as a competitor. It wasn't long before Franklin owned the place and became publisher of *The Pennsylvania Gazette*. Then he started the *Philadelphische Zeitung*, the first foreign language newspaper in the New World. Both papers were incredibly popular and immensely profitable. As he was a master engraver, Franklin had also been hired to print currency for New Jersey, and this led to his appointment as the colony's official printer. Before long he also had contracts to print currency and documents for both Delaware and Pennsylvania. An ordinary man would now have settled back and enjoyed his success.

But Benjamin Franklin was no ordinary man. He took a pen name, Richard Saunders, and began to publish an annual he called *Poor Richard's Almanack*. "I endeavored to make it both entertaining and useful," he said, "and it accordingly came to be in such demand that I reaped considerable profit from it, vending annually near ten thousand. And observing that it was generally read ... scarce any neighborhood in the province being without it ... I considered it was a proper vehicle for conveying instruction among the common people, who bought scarcely any other books. I therefore filled all the little spaces between the remarkable days in the calendar with proverbial sentences, chiefly such as inculcated industry and frugality, as the means of procuring wealth, and thereby securing virtue; it being more difficult for a man in want to act always honestly, as, to use here in one of those proverbs: 'It is hard for an empty sack to stand upright'."

Even though he used a pen name for his almanac, no one was really fooled and Franklin became a very well-known figure around Philadelphia. So it was only natural that he should get involved in public affairs. He began by funding a public library for the city, but this wasn't a completely altruistic act. He himself became the institution's most frequent visitor, using it to expand his education, which had stopped when his apprenticeship ended at the age of ten. His thirst for knowledge was immense, and for years, he said, "reading was the only amusement I allowed myself."

His public career began to blossom when he became Grand Master of Masons in Pennsylvania in 1734, less than a dozen years after his arrival in Philadelphia. Within two more years he was made Clerk of the Assembly of Pennsylvania. Soon after that he became a justice of the peace, and Deputy Postmaster of Philadelphia. The latter eventually led to his appointment as Postmaster General of North America: a post perfectly suited to a newspaper publisher who relied on the mails to distribute his product ... and to expand his influence.

Franklin then began to expand his influence abroad. In 1757, he went to London again, this time as Colonial Agent for the Province of Pennsylvania. During his five years in London he succeeded in breaking the influence of the family of William Penn, who, as proprietors, virtually owned all of Pennsylvania. In the process, he transferred some of their powers to himself. His negotiating skills earned him recognition in the other colonies and he took on the added responsibility of representing Georgia, Massachusetts and New Jersey, as well as Pennsylvania, among the British. When a fight eventually broke out between Britain and her colonies, Benjamin Franklin was in the thick of it. He was on his way home from London on the day the first shots were fired at Lexington and Concord, and when he arrived back at Philadelphia he knew more about the mood in Britain than any other colonial.

It was only natural that he should take a seat in the first Continental Congress, which was held in Philadelphia, and that he should sign the document that its members created: the Declaration of Independence. In fact, Franklin's understanding of the politics involved made him Thomas Jefferson's chief advisor in the wording of the Declaration. Franklin was seventy years old even then, but he lived long enough also to sign the Constitution of the United States, which was drafted in Philadelphia while he was Governor of Pennsylvania. So, of all the men who set America on its course as a nation, it was this Philadelphian, Benjamin Franklin, who signed both the Declaration of Independence and the Constitution, as well as the agreement that made France America's partner in the war and the peace treaty that ended that war.

Not long after the Revolution began, Franklin left Philadelphia again, this time for Paris, where he became America's first ambassador to a foreign country. He was the perfect choice for the job, not so much for his political skills, which were nevertheless prodigious, but

for the fame he had earned abroad as a scientist. In the late 1740s, he took a partner into his printing business so that he could devote more of his time to experiments with electricity. It wasn't exactly a science back then, but there was a great deal of curiosity about what electricity was and whether it might be useful. As the man with the most curious mind in America, it was only natural that Franklin should want to get in on the fun. His contemporaries in the colonies didn't have time for such abstractions, but there were studies going on in England that fascinated him, and building on their knowledge, he discovered that pointed metal objects could attract or repel electrical charges. The theory produced as a result of that discovery was that there are really two kinds of electricity, which Mr. Franklin named "negative" and "positive." This seems like a simple conclusion nowadays, but it was a breakthrough in 1747. Later, his work led him to wonder if lightning might really be charges of electricity. In 1750 he proposed an experiment to draw fire from the sky through a kind of metal sentry box fixed to the top of a tall steeple. There were no steeples tall enough to test his theory in Philadelphia, but when the idea was published in England it was known as "the Philadelphia experiment." The English themselves chose not to risk standing on top of a steeple in a thunderstorm, but in 1752 French scientists took a chance and proved that Franklin was right. British experimenters then confirmed it, and Benjamin Franklin became an international celebrity: he had invented the lightning rod. As it turned out, Franklin had already proved his own theory by hoisting a wire attached to a silk kite into a thundercloud.

At the same time, Franklin was advancing theories on weather patterns, studying population trends, creating mathematical puzzles and even playing with some ideas about raising the dead. He invented a sea anchor to help sailing vessels ride out storms, and charted the course of the Gulf Stream. And he earned the everlasting gratitude of his neighbors by inventing an iron stove that sent the heat into their drafty rooms rather than up the fireplace chimney.

In 1759, his fame as a scientist earned him an honorary doctorate from the Scottish University of St. Andrews and the title stood him in good stead in his role as a diplomat from a country that was scrupulously avoiding titles. But in spite of his accomplishments and the honors that had been heaped on his head, he never changed the epitaph he had written for himself as a young man. It reads: "The Body of Benjamin Franklin, Printer, (Like the cover of an old book, its contents torn out and stript of its lettering & gilding) lies here, food for the worms. Yet the work itself shall not be lost; for it will (as he believed) appear once more, in a new and more beautiful edition, corrected and amended by the Author."

Franklin's influence on Philadelphia was so profound that one of his contemporaries said "no other town burying its great man ever buried more of itself than Philadelphia with Franklin." But the town itself had provided the right opportunity for the great man to blossom. Credit for that goes to its founder, William Penn, the most enlightened of all the colonial proprietors in America.

Penn's father was an admiral in the British Navy and he commanded the ship that carried Charles II back to England when the monarchy was restored in 1660. The act earned him a knighthood, and the King's eternal friendship. Admiral Penn wanted his son, William, to have a career in politics and in a way he got his wish, even though the young man really wanted to be soldier. But William's plan was sidetracked when he met the Quakers and decided to become one himself. Among other indignities aimed at the Society of Friends, England had a law forbidding more than five Quakers to gather together "under the pretext of worship." As the prominent son of a famous man, Penn was closely watched, and when he was seen at a Quaker meeting, he was arrested and tossed into the Tower of London to reconsider his decision to join the nonconformists. Instead, he used the time to strengthen his resolve and to develop a plan for the future.

Penn's plan, he said, was a "holy experiment." And its future was in a place he would call Philadelphia. He also found time to write a pamphlet pleading his own case, which impressed the King and secured his release. Before long he was arrested again for helping other imprisoned Quakers, but was acquitted by the jury. The furious judge ordered all twelve jurors to be arrested for contempt of court, and Penn took on their case. It went all the way to the highest court in England where the Lord Chief Justice ruled, in a landmark decision that is now a basic part of common law in both England and the United States, that the members of a jury may never be punished for the jury's verdict.

By now Penn was more than ready to begin his "holy experiment" and petitioned the King for a grant of land in the New World. The grant of more than twenty-eight million acres made William Penn the largest landowner in North America, after King Charles himself. The King attached the name Penn to the grant to honor his friend the Admiral, but the new proprietor thought it was too vain, especially for a Quaker, to name the colony for his family. He countered with a suggestion that it be called "New Wales," because the family had roots in Wales and the new countryside resembled that country more than any other part of the British Isles. When the King rejected that idea, Penn countered with "Sylvania," a fancy word for "woodland." The King nodded his head in agreement, but took out his quill and added the letters P-E-N-N to the front of it. Then he waved the young man away. The discussion was over.

When Penn arrived at the site of his new colony in 1682, he chose a spot on the Delaware River with a small harbor and a beach with high land above on which to build what he had visualized as a "green country town." He ordered that all the streets should be straight and orderly and leading toward the harbor, where he wanted a commercial center built. He asked home builders to center their houses so there would be room on all sides for orchards and gardens, not to mention protection from the fires which were the bane of existence in cities all over the world.

He set his "holy experiment" in motion by telling settlers that he wanted them to be governed by laws of their own making. But he also gave them what he called the Great Law, which, among other things, said that "No person shall be molested or prejudiced for his or her conscientious persuasion or practice. Nor shall he or she at any time be compelled to frequent or maintain any religious worship, place or ministry whatever, contrary to his or her mind."

Other colonies had been established in America long before Penn set foot on the shores of the Delaware River, and most of them professed to have religious freedom at the core of their belief. But this was the first that didn't reserve freedom for one religion to the exclusion of others. Even more important, William Penn was the first to refer to the citizens of his colony using the words "his or her."

Penn's attitude toward the Indians was just as revolutionary. It was so enlightened, they called him "brother" almost immediately. But Penn said, "I will not call you children or brothers only; for parents are apt to whip their children, and brothers sometimes will differ." He told them he considered them to be the same flesh and blood as the Christians. Even before leaving England, Penn had written a letter to the Shawnee, Iroquois and Lenni Lenape chiefs, which he signed "I am your loving friend." He proved it by signing a treaty with them pledging good faith and friendship "as long as the creeks and rivers run, and while the sun, moon and stars endure." In the years ahead other white men would make the same promises, but though neither side thought it necessary to formalize this one, beyond recording that a meeting had taken place, the French philosopher Voltaire would later marvel that it was the only treaty in the history of the world never sworn to and yet never broken. As the colony grew, people living in remote areas thought nothing of leaving their children in the care of Indians when they were not at home and the native Americans walked the streets of Philadelphia without fear, and without creating fear.

In all, Penn lived in Pennsylvania for only three years. He spent most of the rest of his life in England, straightening out conflicting land grants and promoting settlement in Pennsylvania. When he died in England in 1718, his Quaker neighbors wrote that his work in America "will be valued by the wise and blessed with the just." From Pennsylvania itself, the Indian chiefs sent his widow skins "to make a garment suitable for traveling through a thorny wilderness without your guide."

His work to colonize Pennsylvania extended into Germany, where he promised hard-working farmers a better life. He went to his ancestral home of Wales, and names like Penlyn and Bryn Athyn were added to the map of his colony. Scotch-Irish emigrated from Northern Ireland, and over time they have been joined by Italians, Blacks, Chinese and others who have proved that Philadelphia is, indeed, the City of Brotherly Love. It has been called the most American of American cities, and this statement has nothing to do with the fact that America's roots are here. No matter what their ethnic roots, everyone in the city considers themselves Philadelphians first and foremost. The mixture works better in Pennsylvania's southeast corner than almost anywhere else in the United States. It's what William Penn dreamed would happen, and what Benjamin Franklin found so much to his liking.

*Facing page: a recumbent moose surveys the city from the Washington Fountain.*

*Well-kept hedges outside the huge Philadelphia Museum of Art (below left), one of the most important museums of its kind in the East. Above, above left and overleaf: No. 1 Liberty Plaza, designed by Helmut Jahn and reminiscent of New York's Chrysler Building. This skyscraper rises nearly a thousand feet above the city, thereby breaking Philadelphia's unwritten rule that no building should rise higher than the tower of City Hall (below and facing page). Left: traffic at the intersection of Broad Street and Market Street at dusk.*

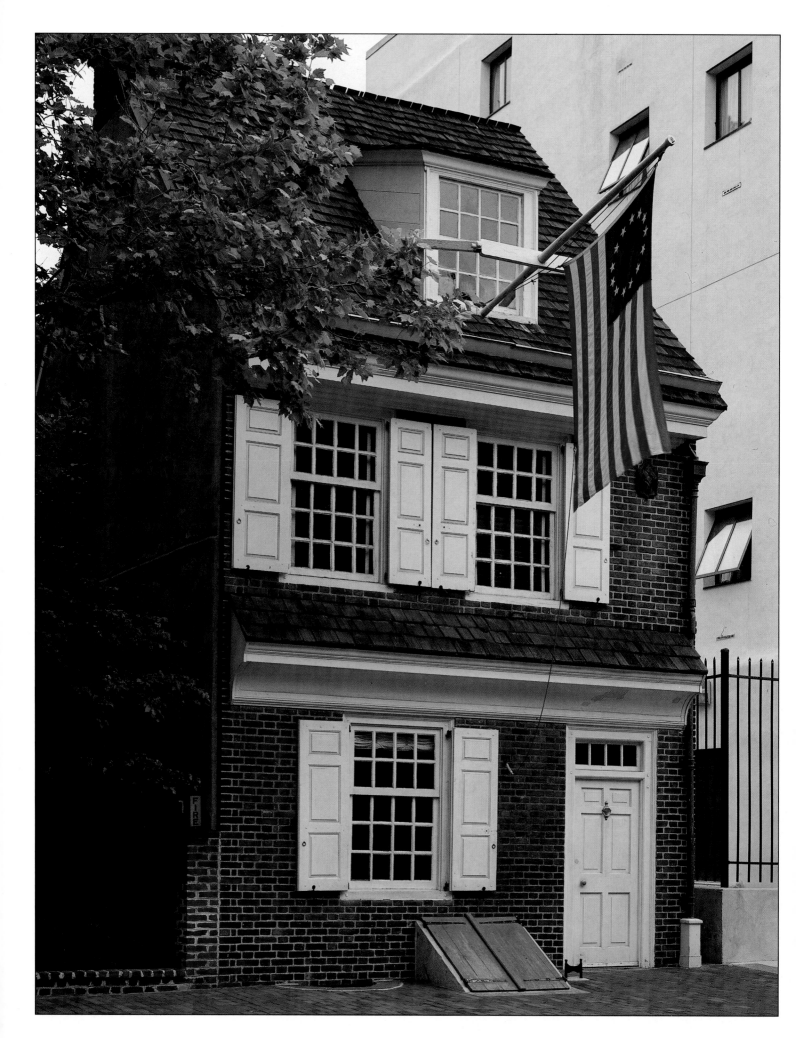

*Facing page: Betsy Ross House on Arch Street, the home of the seamstress who first sewed the Stars and Stripes flag. Above: Carpenters' Hall in Independence National Historical Park and (below) Independence Hall, the centerpiece of the park. The Hall contains the Assembly Room (above right), where the Declaration of Independence was signed. The Pennsylvania Supreme Court Chamber (overleaf) is also in the building. Below right: the glass pavilion where the Liberty Bell (right) hangs in Independence National Historical Park.*

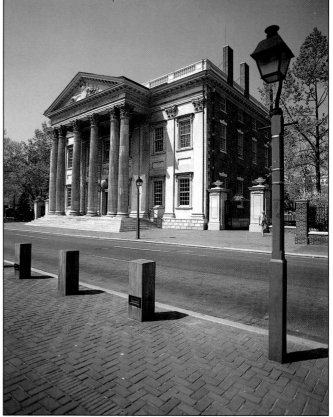

*Above and facing page: the First Bank of the United States and (below and below left) the Second Bank. Both were built when Philadelphia was the financial capital of the nation, but neither building serves as a bank today. Above left: the Philadelphia Exchange, a nineteenth-century building now fully restored and part of Independence National Historical Park, and (left) the Free Library of Philadelphia on Logan Square. Overleaf: the steps of the Philadelphia Museum of Art, where Silvester Stallone trained in the film "Rocky."*

Above left: Carpenters' Hall, built by the Carpenters' Company in 1770 and later used by the First Continental Congress. Above and left: Franklin Court; girders mark where Ben Franklin's house once stood. Overleaf: the Market Street Houses that stand in front of Franklin's home and were built by him to let. Below left: the "A Man Full of Trouble" Tavern, (below) Elfreth's Alley and (facing page top) the Stars and Stripes outside Powel House, home of a former Philadelphian mayor. Facing page bottom: Head House Square.

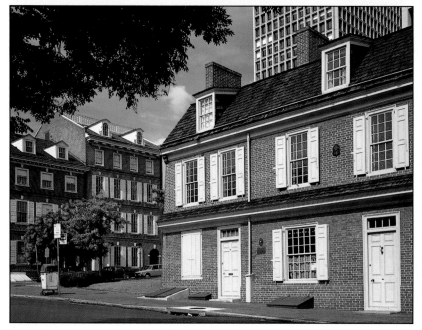

*Facing page top, above right and right: Mount Pleasant, built by the Philadelphian privateer Captain John MacPherson in 1761. Benedict Arnold purchased the mansion in 1779 as a wedding gift for his bride Peggy Shippen, but because of the charges of treason against him both were obliged to flee to England before they could live in the house. A later owner was a great-nephew of Benjamin Franklin, Jonathan Williams, the first superintendent of West Point. MacPherson commissioned the finest craftsmen of the day to carve the woodwork at Mount Pleasant and the house also boasts some superb eighteenth-century furnishings, fine china and several notable paintings. Facing page bottom, above, below and below right: Cedar Grove, a Quaker farmhouse in Fairmount Park that dates back to 1748, but which was substantially enlarged fifty years after that date. The front of the house is built of regular stone, the sides of irregular stone and the back of brick. Its unusually fine collection of Jacobean, Queen Anne, William and Mary, Chippendale and Federal furniture was assembled by five generations of the Quaker Paschall-Morris family to whom Cedar Grove was home. Prior to 1927 the house stood in the Northern Liberties and served as a quiet country retreat, but as the district around it became more populated, the family had the house dismantled stone by stone and re-erected in Fairmount Park. In effect, the country retreat had retreated!*

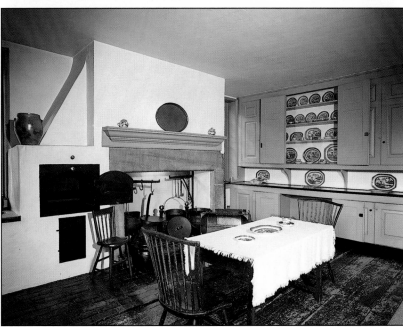

*These pages and overleaf: Strawberry Mansion, the largest mansion open to the public in Fairmount Park. The first house on the site was built in the 1750s, but, since it belonged to a member of the Continental Congress, the English burned it down in the Revolutionary War. The second house was known as Somerville; the present name dates from 1842, when a Mrs. Grimes lived here and sold strawberries to visitors.*

*Facing page: frogs spew forth jets of water towards reclining nudes and swans in the Swan Memorial Fountain, the centerpiece of Logan Circle on the Benjamin Franklin Parkway (below). Logan Circle is named for the secretary of Penn, William Logan, once Chief Justice of Pennsylvania.*

*These pages and overleaf: Penn's Landing, a thirty-seven-acre riverfront development that boasts a fleet of historical vessels. Facing page top and below: the 1907* Moshulu, *the largest steel sailing ship in the world, (facing page bottom, above right and below right) the cruiser USS* Olympia *and the submarine USS* Becuna *and (above and right) the* Gazela Primeiro, *the last of the square-rigged Portugese fishing ships. Overleaf: the 1904 iron* Lightship Number 79 *that illuminated the shipping lanes of Philadelphia for over sixty years.*

*These pages: fountains and mobiles decorate Gallery Mall on Market Street. This modern complex contains 125 stores. The Philadelphia Bourse (overleaf) on Fifth Street was built between 1893 and 1895 and once included an exhibition hall and a stock exchange. Today it houses shops and offices.*

*Facing page and above: spring in the walled Eighteenth-Century Garden on Walnut Street, an English garden that exhibits species of trees, shrubs and flowers typical of those grown in the city prior to 1800. Maintained by the Pennsylvania Horticultural Society, it is part of Independence National Historical Park, as is Franklin Court (below) and the Greek Revival Second Bank of America (below right). Remaining pictures: tulips brighten the extensive flowerbeds of Logan Circle on the Benjamin Franklin Parkway.*

*Above and left: beautifully proportioned, eighteenth-century Laurel Hill mansion, a former home of Mayor Samuel Shoemaker. Above left: the Carriage House of the estate of Baleroy mansion. A portrait of a former Lord Mayor of London hangs in the reception room (below) of this house, while the dining room (below left) displays chairs used by the signatories of the Declaration of Independence. Facing page: Sweetbriar mansion, built beside the Schuylkill River soon after the marriage of the owner, Samuel Breck, in 1795.*

*The highlight of a tour of Independence Hall is the Assembly Room (below left), where American independence from Britain was declared on July 4, 1776. Jefferson's walking cane is displayed on one of the desks, and Washington's chair can also be seen. Also open to the public are the Senate Chamber (below), the Pennsylvania Supreme Court Chamber (left) and the Governor's Council Chamber (bottom left).*

*Facing page top: a permanently burning flame on the Tomb of the Unknown Soldier of the American Revolution, Washington Square. Facing page bottom: the interior of Christ Church on Second Street, (below) the Franklin Memorial in the Franklin Institute and (overleaf) the Pennsylvania Academy of Fine Art.*

The elaborate pediment of the north wing of the Philadelphia Museum of Modern Art (above and above left) illustrates the theme of sacred and profane love. Apparently not enough money was found to decorate the central and south buildings similarly. Left: a copy of Rodin's The Thinker outside the Rodin Museum and (below left) the city's Grecian-style Old Philadelphia Waterworks. Below: the equestrian bronze of the first President that surmounts the Washington Fountain (facing page) in Fairmount Park (overleaf).

The Woodford Mansion (these pages and overleaf) in Fairmount Park was built by merchant William Coleman in 1756. It contains the Naomi Wood Collection of Colonial household equipment – considered to be the best of its kind in America. The mansion remains virtually unchanged since the days when Benjamin Franklin and other important dignitaries ate in the dining room (above). The kitchen (facing page bottom) is particularly noteworthy as it contains a rare collection of Pennsylvanian Dutch ware and furniture.